DESMOND DIGS DINOSAURS

Published Internationally by Publisher Services,
65 E Wacker Pl., Chicago, IL 60601

© Cara P Fucci 2018

Terms and Conditions:
The purchser of this book is subject to the condition
that he/she shall in no way resell it,
nor any part of it, nor make copies of it to distribute freely.

All Person Fictitious Disclaimer:
This book is a work of fiction. Any similarity betwen the characters
and situations within its pages and places or persons, living or dead,
is unintentional and co-incidental.

DESMOND LOVES HIS DINOSAURS

HE KNOWS ALL ABOUT THEM.

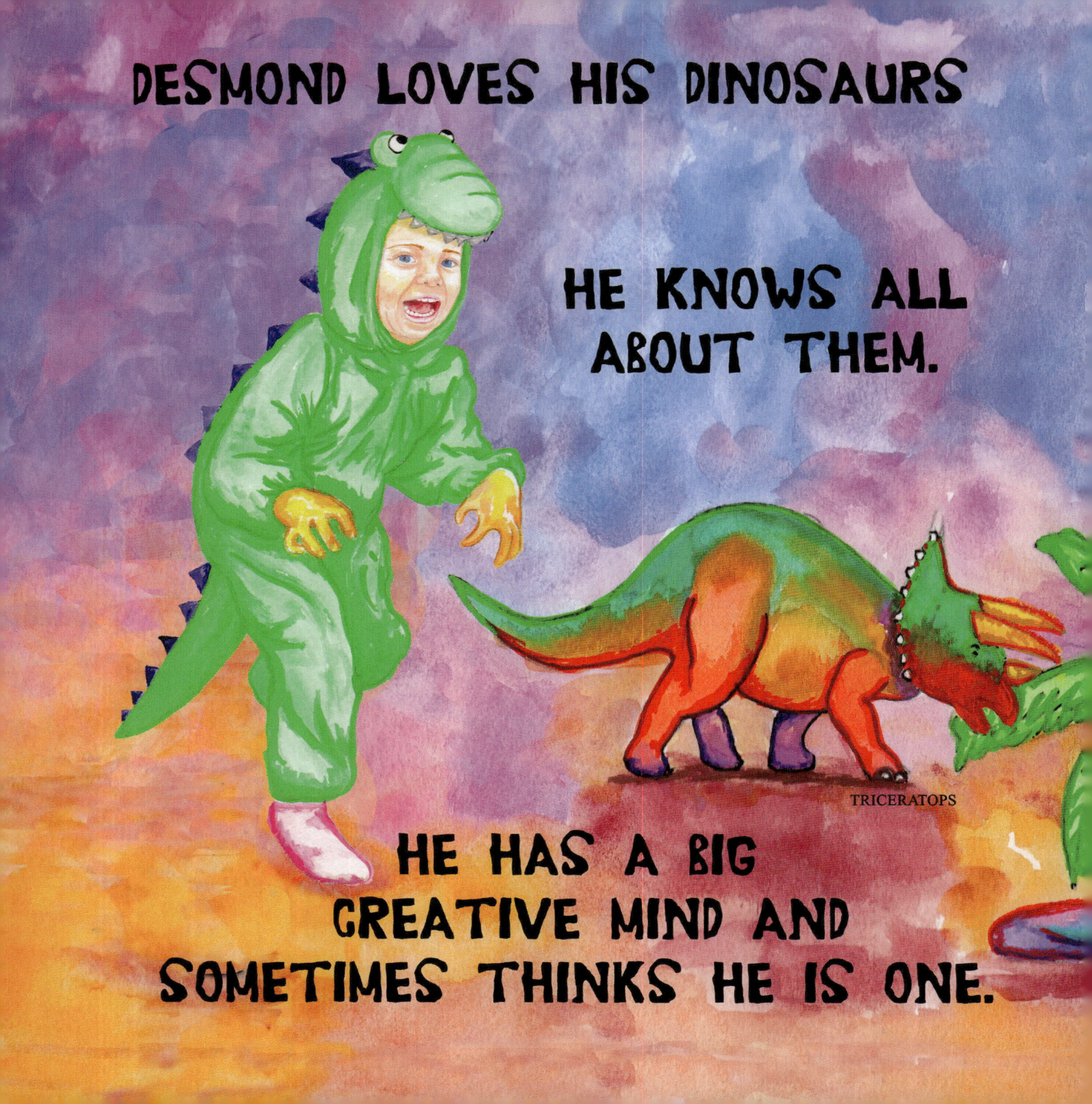

HE HAS A BIG CREATIVE MIND AND SOMETIMES THINKS HE IS ONE.

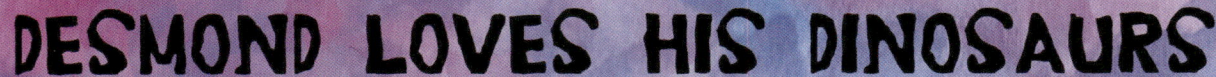

IGUANODONS AND DIPLODOCUS

DIPLODOCUS

IGUANODON

DINOSAURS OF DIFFERENT SIZES.

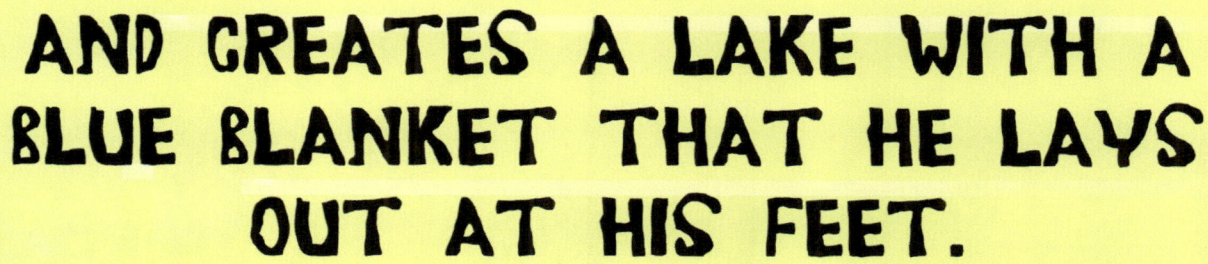

AND CREATES A LAKE WITH A BLUE BLANKET THAT HE LAYS OUT AT HIS FEET.

HE STOMPS AROUND AND MAKES A ROAR AND GNASHES HIS BIG TEETH.

DES SAYS, "I'M THE FIERCEST DINOSAUR AND IT'S TIME FOR ME TO EAT!"

Desmond clomps across the floor, roaring and lifting his feet.

"Now I am a carnivore and looking for meat to eat!"

THEN CRAWLS UP THE MOUND
TO THE TOP OF THE PILE
FEELING QUITE NOURISHED.

ANOTHER ROAR COMES FROM HIS MOUTH AS HE TUMBLES DOWN THE MOUND,

LANDING IN THE ROUND SAND PIT HE CREATED ON THE GROUND.

THEN HIS MOM POPS IN THE ROOM
TO SAY IT'S DINNERTIME.

DESMOND'S TUMMY HAD BEGUN
TO GROWL,
SHE CAME IN THE NICK OF TIME.

ALL THE PRETENDING HE HAD DONE, MADE DESMOND'S TUMMY ROAR.

DESMOND WAS QUITE READY TO EAT NUGGETS SHAPED LIKE DINOSAURS!

"YOUR DINO-NUGGETS ARE GETTING COLD," MOM SAYS WITH A SMILE. THINKING OF HIS FAVORITE FOOD MADE STOPPING PLAY WORTHWHILE.

"BUT FIRST," MOM SAYS, "PLEASE CLEAN THIS ROOM BEFORE COMING DOWNSTAIRS."

"OKAY", DES SIGHS AND THEN UNDOES THE WORLD HE HAD PREPARED.

AND KNEW THAT ALL THE ROARS
WOULD HAVE TO
WAIT ANOTHER DAY.

Printed in Great Britain
by Amazon